Cut The Credit Card Debt

Eliminate Debt By Stopping Your Credit Card Addiction

Table of Contents

Introduction 3

Chapter 1: Learning The Basics Of Credit Cards 5

Chapter 2: The Exorbitant Rates Of Credit Cards ... 11

Chapter 3: Warning Signs Of Credit Card Addiction 14

Chapter 4: Negative Effects Of Credit Card Addiction And Having Debt...18

Chapter 5: Short-Term Solutions To Stop Credit Card Addiction 25

Chapter 6: Long-Term Solutions To Stop Credit Card Addiction..33

Chapter 7: More Tips For Paying Off Your Credit Card Debt..37

Chapter 8: Improving Your Credit Without Credit Cards

Conclusion 40

Introduction

I want to thank you and congratulate you for purchasing the book, *"Cut The Credit Card Debt: Eliminate Debt by Stopping Your Credit Card Addiction"*.

This book contains proven steps and strategies on how to stop your credit card addiction and eliminate debt.

Many people in the U.S. use credit cards to make purchases. Some are even required to open a credit card account that can help them build their credit and allow them to apply for loans such as car loans and house loans. Credit cards are useful for almost all kinds of transactions like buying groceries, booking a flight, paying for hospital bills, and many more. You cannot deny the fact that credit cards are important in today's society, especially if you want to use a more convenient way of paying for your transactions. Credit cards can also build your credit and help you live a comfortable life.

However, credit cards have gained a notorious reputation because many people find it difficult to control their spending knowing that they can use their credit card and pay for their purchases later. It can be addictive because it gives you the power to purchase even if you do not have cash in your wallet. It gives you the thrill of being able to purchase something that you really want to buy and worrying about the payment later. This is where credit card addiction begins.

When a person uses their credit card flagrantly, without thinking if they can pay for the balance with their income, they will find themselves in debt, which may lead to bankruptcy. This is something that you do not want to happen. You need to stop your credit card addiction right away and be debt-free.

You will learn more about credit card usage, high interest rates, negative effects of having excessive debts and warning signs of credit card addiction throughout this book. You will also learn some tips and strategies for treating your credit card addiction and eliminate debt for good.

Thanks again for purchasing this book, I hope you enjoy it!

Chapter 1: Learning The Basics Of Credit Cards

People have varying opinions when it comes to credit cards. Ask people you know and they will give you different answers. Some people think that credit cards are among man's greatest creations because these cards helped them in times of financial emergencies. Others also think that these plastic cards are used by the devil itself to make people become more materialistic by buying things that their income cannot afford and ending up in bankruptcy.

These varying opinions are not only observed among ordinary individuals who own or used to own credit cards, but also among financial experts who have a deeper understanding of how credit cards work. Some experts believe that with the right usage, credit cards can make a person's life more comfortable by improving their credit history. Others, on the other hand, believe in the destructive power of having a credit card in your wallet, causing them to promote the importance of living a debt-free life.

The truth is that credit cards are nothing more than inanimate objects. They are not inherently bad or good. Just like guns, the effects of credit cards depend on the knowledge and skills of the person using it. If a person knows the ins and outs of credit cards and knows how to use them the right way, then he will most likely get positive benefits from using them. On the other hand, someone who has a limited view of credit cards and thinks of them as tools that can be used to purchase things when they do not have the cash to pay for them will most likely end up with a lot of debt. Many people just decide not to own credit cards to avoid the temptation of buying things that they really cannot afford.

To understand more about the basics of credit cards, read on!

What are credit cards?

Everyone knows what a credit card looks like. For those who have been living under a rock and have no idea what a credit card looks like, here is a physical description. Credit cards are thin rectangular cards that are usually made of plastic, thus the nickname "plastic" when referring to a credit card. They can also be sometimes made of metallic alloy or graphite, depending on the company issuing them.

At the back of these cards, you will find a magnetic strip. Some cards also have a small RFID chip that can usually be found on one side of the card. All credit cards also indicate the name of the account holder, whether it is a person's name or a company name, the expiry date, and the account number.

A credit card is a lot more than a small rectangular piece of plastic. It represents the credit card account that you have opened under your chosen bank. When using the credit card, it is like you are borrowing the bank's money when making a purchase, with the promise to pay back a partial or full amount on or before the due date. Since you are borrowing money from the bank, you need to pay a certain amount of interest. This is how lending works in almost all financial institutions or even between individuals and this is how banks earn money from credit cards.

Spending other people's money to buy things instead of your own is where the acquisition of debts begins. If you use your credit card to make purchases and use your income for other purposes, then what are you going to use to pay for the balance in your credit card plus the interest? This is how people get up to their eyeballs in debt. They forget the fact that they still need to pay for their purchases at a later date, together with the interest.

How do they work?

You can use credit cards to pay for almost any purchases and transactions. Once you have decided on what you want to buy and the cashier has punched in all the items, you can now present your credit card to the cashier who will then validate your account online using a secure Internet connection. To validate your account, the cashier has to swipe your credit card through a machine and the merchant is the one who will validate the account.

The bank will also accept or reject the purchase. A purchase will not go through if you have reached your credit limit or if there is a hold on your credit card. However, if everything is okay, the purchase will go through and it will then be added to the list of other purchases you have made using the same credit card.

The cashier is not the only one responsible for validating your card, although it may seem like it because he is the one in front of you holding your credit card. When your card is swiped, different companies are involved and money is being passed through from one company to another.

You can see all your credit card purchases for the month by checking your monthly statement. The best way to deal with your statement is to pay it in full on or before the due date no matter what to avoid late fees and accumulated interest. When you make a habit of paying only the minimum, you can avoid the late fee, but your debt will become larger and larger because of the interest that keeps accumulating every month.

With the accumulating interest, a purchase worth $50 can become $100 or more. This is also how people end up being bankrupt: when the interest needing to be paid on their credit card is a lot larger than the amount of their original purchase. The lesson here is to pay your credit card in full and on time. The high interest rates of credit cards are important factors in acquiring debt, which is why they will be discussed in detail in a separate chapter.

Banks see you as a well-behaved customer if you always pay your account in full and on time. They will report this to the credit bureaus that give individuals a credit score. A high credit score means a good financial history. This can have a lot of consequences in the future, like when applying for a loan, finding a rental place to stay, or even looking for a job. Companies and individuals prefer to deal with someone who has a good credit history because it means that the person is responsible, especially in paying bills on time.

However, you need to keep in mind that banks prefer customers who are not late, but pay only a partial amount of their balance, because this is where they get their profits. If you pay in full all the time, you do not give the bank a chance to apply the interest rate. This is why, in reality, banks want you to spend more and more using your credit card, even if you do not have money to pay for your purchases in full. They want to profit from you by only paying the minimum due and accruing more and more interest.

Why do people cut their cards?

You have probably heard of people cutting up their cards or putting them in the freezer. They do this to avoid the temptation of using their credit cards. It is easier to buy something using your credit card than actual cash because actual cash is scarce and people are more likely to think twice before spending their cash. It is easily noticeable when you have no cash left in your wallet.

On the other hand, you only get to see your credit card statement once a month. Some people even intentionally do not open their credit card statements when they know that they will only see the large debt that they have accumulated. People tend to conserve cash more because they can easily see when they are running out of it, unlike credit cards.

People also cut their credit cards because these plastics only make them spend more money than they actually earn. For example, if a person earns $10,000 a month and their credit limit is $15,000, they can go beyond spending $10,000 and spend all the $15,000 on their credit card, because it is still allowed by the bank. This will put them at $5,000 worth of credit. This will be the start of acquiring

Cut The Credit Card Debt

more and more debt until the person no longer knows how to pay for it. This means more profit for the bank and more debt for the individual.

These are the basics that you need to know about credit cards. The next chapter will discuss the high interest rates of credit cards and how they can make a person acquire too much debt that they cannot afford to pay.

Chapter 2: The Exorbitant Rates Of Credit Cards

According to research conducted by IndexCreditCards.com, the average credit card balance among households was $7,394 in 2010. The average interest rate of credit cards ranges from a whopping 17% to 20%. No wonder so many people have a hard time paying off their credit cards! This is the main reason why some people just decide to cut up their credit cards so that they can no longer use them to make purchases that will double the amount because of the interest rates. It can be very difficult for people to pay off their credit card debt with these exorbitant interest rates.

The interest rate is synonymous with annual percentage rate. This amount of money is what you need to pay for having the privilege of using someone else's money, in this case, the bank's money. This is how banks earn profits from their credit card account holders. If you have a credit card, then it gives you the privilege to spend an amount of money today that would otherwise take you weeks to earn and save up. If you flip the coin and look at the other side, the bank is lending you money that it could otherwise spend today, which is why banks require interest and fee to compensate for this loss of opportunity to spend money. Time is an essential factor in determining the interest and value of money.

Credit cards are an important part of an average household's day-to-day life. In fact, total debts acquired using credit cards have reached $2.43 trillion as of May 2011. This shows how dependent

Cut The Credit Card Debt

Americans are on their credit cards. This also shows the high level of consumerism in the country. It is important that you understand how using credit cards can make you go bankrupt and how the interest rates play a significant role in your overall debt.

Let's take a look at this scenario. Mary has a $2,000 balance on her credit card with 20% annual percentage rate (APR). The minimum payment each month is $10 or 3%, whichever is higher. Mary only pays the minimum, which is $60, or 3% of the balance.

To compute how the payment is broken down to pay for the principal loan and interest, you need to divide the APR by 12 to get your monthly interest rate. In this case, it will be 20%÷12, which is equal to 1.66%. Multiply $2,000 by 1.666% and you will get $33.33, which is the interest that your account accrued in a month. Mary paid $60 as the minimum payment.

Subtract the interest $33.33 from $60 and you will get $26.67, which is the amount that will be deducted from the principal loan amount $2,000. So if Mary pays $60 for the month, her remaining total balance will be $1,973.33. You can do the same computation every month until Mary pays off the balance on her credit card in full.

With this computation, Mary will be able to pay off her account in full after 15 years and the total amount will be $4,240, which includes the principal loan of $2,000 and the interest rates. This means that the interest is $2,240, which is actually $240 higher than the original loan amount.

Cut The Credit Card Debt

If Mary adds $10 on top of her $60 minimum payment, she will be able to pay off her credit card debt in over seven years for a total of $3,276. This means that by just adding $10 every month on her payment, Mary can save $964 and it can cut the time that she needs to pay off her account in half.

This shows how a small credit card debt can double in amount over the years when you only pay the minimum. Every single dollar counts and it is not advisable to pay only the minimum, or even an amount that is only slightly higher than your minimum. It is best not to carry balance in your credit card at all, or better yet, just cut your credit card in half so that you have no chance of ending up in this dire financial situation.

Chapter 3: Warning Signs Of Credit Card Addiction

Is there such a thing as credit card addiction? Can someone really be addicted to using these plastics that have exorbitant interest rates? The answer to both of these questions is "Yes". Credit card addiction and compulsive shopping are interrelated, because many compulsive shoppers use their credit cards to pay for their purchases. This is depicted in the movie *Confessions of a Shopaholic*, where the heroine is a compulsive buyer who ends up acquiring too much debt on her credit cards. The situation looks funny in the movie, but having a lot of debt that you have no way of paying can get you in a lot of trouble in real life.

Credit card addiction is the overwhelming desire to buy things that you may or may not need using your credit card. This can potentially ruin your finances in the end, because when your debt starts to build up, your income will no longer be enough to pay for it and you will end up bankrupt. Compulsive shoppers use credit cards to feed their shopping obsession. This is because it is more difficult to spend hard-earned cash that you have in your wallet than to spend borrowed money contained in a plastic card.

To be able to treat your credit card addiction and eliminate debt, you first need to know if you really have the condition. You need to observe your credit card usage to identify potential red flags that could mean shopping addiction using your credit card. If you can observe any of these warning signs, you may be suffering from credit card addiction:

Cut The Credit Card Debt

- Frequently buying things that you do not really need is one red flag that you need to look out for. Because of this, you end up with a lot of stuff at home that you do not really use and only end up collecting dust at the back of your closet or under your bed. You are also tempted to buy unnecessary items just because they are on sale.
- When you hide your purchases from your spouse, parents, or other close family members, it could also be a sign that you have credit card addiction because you know that what you are doing is not something to be proud of. You know that you are doing something wrong, which gives you that guilty feeling and is the reason why you hide your purchases.
- Another warning sign is when most or all of your credit cards are maxed out, which means that you have reached your credit cards' limit and you can no longer use them to make purchases unless you pay at least the minimum.
- You are also in trouble if you just keep on paying the minimum every month. As has been explained in the previous chapter, paying the minimum prevents you from getting a late fee, but what it actually does is it doubles the balance that you need to pay.

You also need to watch out for other less acute warning signs that can ultimately lead you to a lot of debt. Check out the list below:

- Using your credit card to purchase everyday items, even those that only cost a few dollars, is also an indication of a possible credit card

addiction. Paying for small groceries, gas, dollar meals, a pack of cigarettes, and other inexpensive items is not a good idea because once these items add up, you will realize that you have already acquired a lot of debt without buying anything major.
- Not paying your full balance every month can also lead to credit card addiction because it gives you the feeling that you can get away with not paying the full balance. Later on, you will only pay the minimum and before you know it, you have accumulated a large debt on your credit card.
- People who ignore their credit card statements because they are afraid to look at their bill also display signs of credit card addiction. This means that you have done something that has dire consequences, which is why you are afraid to view your credit card statement.
- When you are juggling several credit card bills, and you are skipping one bill to pay off another, or you are making cash advances from one credit card to pay another, then it is possible that you have credit card addiction.
- Some people also rely heavily on their credit cards to pay for things that are not in their budget. This can also be a sign of credit card addiction. For example, if a designer bag is definitely not in your budget because you cannot afford it with your income, but you are still going to buy it because you have a credit card.
- Another sign that indicates that you are heading towards credit card addiction is when you have several past due accounts. This means that you have been using your credit

- cards, but have not been able to pay even for the minimum fee.
- There are also those who are habitual buyers and returners. They buy things compulsively only to return the items the next day because once they arrived home, they realize that they do not really need or like the item. They just cannot control their urge to shop using their credit card.
- There is also a condition called "retail therapy" where people, go shopping to make themselves feel better when they are in a negative mood. If you are like this, then you should be wary of your behavior because this can be a sign of credit card addiction or compulsive shopping.

Once you have assessed your behavior involving your credit cards and realized that you actually have credit card addiction, the first thing that you need to do is to calm down and not panic. You need to understand that this problem is common and you are not alone. There are also a lot of ways that you can stop your credit card addiction and eliminate your debt for good. These will be discussed in the next few chapters.

However, for now, you need to understand the negative effects of credit card addiction and compulsive shopping on your physical and mental health, emotions, relationships, career and life in general.

Chapter 4: Negative Effects Of Credit Card Addiction And Having Debt

It goes without saying that credit card addiction and debt have negative effects. Anything in excess is not good, as they always say. You need to learn about the negative effects of acquiring debt using your credit card so that you can understand why it is extremely important to stop this addiction and get rid of your debts.

If you think that credit card addiction and debt only has an effect on your finances, then you are wrong, because this problem affects many different aspects of your life. You may feel a thrill and excitement because you are able to buy things that you otherwise cannot afford if you just depend on your income, but using your credit card excessively has dire consequences in the end.

As you are using up the credit in your cards and you keep on ignoring your bills, your debt increases together with the interest, which can have a lot of negative effects on your life. Some negative effects of credit card addiction and having debt are direct, while others are side effects. It is like a disease that can have complications when not treated properly and right away. Many people say that money is the root of all evil. You will have a deeper understanding of this saying when you find yourself way in over your head with debt.

Here are some negative direct and side effects of credit card addiction and having debt that you need to know about.

Effects on your physical health

Stress is one of the main effects of having a credit card addiction that you need to hide from your loved ones. When you feel stressed out, your immune system weakens which makes you more prone to different kinds of diseases. Worrying too much can also lead to high blood pressure. High blood pressure can cause heart attacks and stroke.

Aside from these direct effects, having a huge credit card debt can also have side effects. You cannot afford nutritious foods, enroll in a gym class, buy supplements, or have a regular checkup if you are in debt because you have probably used up your savings. It also affects your physical appearance because stress makes you look older than your age. It causes wrinkles, dry skin, brittle hair, and acne that can negatively affect your appearance. It may sound vain and shallow, but your physical appearance plays an important role in boosting your confidence.

Effects on emotional and mental health

Your credit card addiction and debt can also be detrimental to your emotional and mental health. You will experience a rollercoaster of emotions that can lead to mental and emotional breakdown, especially if you are the type of person who cannot handle too much stress. Here are some emotions that you may experience when you find yourself in a negative financial situation:

- ***Denial.*** Initially, you will be in denial because you simply cannot accept the fact that you have allowed yourself to lose control of your spending and gotten yourself into the situation that you are in. You will ignore the red flags that are waving in front of you, like your daily credit card purchases, over the limit accounts, and late payments. You just keep on fooling yourself and continue making purchases using your credit card. You will only stop being in denial when an outside occurrence like legal action, a visit or call from a bill collector, or a rejected transaction forces you to face your problem and start making changes in your credit card usage and spending habits.

- **Fear and panic.** You will also experience fear and panic when faced with a large credit card bill. Just imagine how you would feel if you receive your credit card statement and found out that your balance is $20,000 and you are only earning $8,000 a month without any other sources of income. You will surely feel fear and panic because you have no idea how you are going to pay off your debt and you are wondering when the bill collectors will start calling you. You will also be afraid when your partner finds out about your financial situation, especially if you have been hiding your purchases. You will panic when you realize that you have just used up your savings for your kids' education that you and your partner have spent years saving up for.

- **Anger.** Anger is another emotion that you will feel when you are in a tight financial situation. You will be angry with yourself for losing control over your spending and credit card usage. You will be angry with your company for giving you a low salary. You will be angry with the credit card companies for their high interest rate.

You will be angry with the people around you and you will find yourself picking fights and being in a dark cloud every day. You will be angry at the world when in fact, you have no one else to blame but yourself. You need to be careful when it comes to anger because this can lead to something more serious like crime and violence.

- **Depression.** A person may feel depressed when all these negative emotions build up and when the situation becomes too overwhelming. Depression may lead to emotional and mental breakdown or even suicide. In fact, financial problems are one of the main causes of suicide throughout the history of humankind. Some people also cope with depression and their financial problem by drinking alcohol or using drugs.

    When you start to feel hopeless about your situation, as if you have given up on everything, you need to talk to someone close to you or go to a professional who can help you with what you are going through. Keep in mind that there are numerous solutions to your problem and giving up on life is not one of them.

Effects on family and relationships

Excessive use of credit card and acquiring too much debt can also have negative effects on your family and relationships. Your partner or spouse may lose his or her trust in you, especially if you keep your credit card shopping a secret by hiding your purchases and credit card statements. Some couples even end up getting a divorce when they find themselves in an unhappy financial situation caused by one of them. Your whole family will also suffer because you are not saving up money for important things such as your family's basic needs, your mortgage, your kids' education, and so on.

Your children may resent you when they have to make adjustments and changes in their lives caused by your excessive spending. There are also those who withdraw from their friends because they feel embarrassed about their situation. They do not want their friends to find out that they really cannot afford their lavish lifestyle or the expensive things that they often purchase.

Effects on career

Your job may also be affected if you have debt or credit card addiction. People who are addicted to shopping using their credit card sometimes cannot keep themselves from browsing online shops to see what they can buy, even when they are at work. People who have a huge debt may also be tempted to embezzle money from their company, especially if they are responsible for their company's finances. These scenarios can lead to termination of employment, which will look bad in your professional record.

Unpaid debts will reflect on your credit history. You might not get the job that you are applying for, especially if it is related to money, if you have a poor credit history, because it shows that you cannot handle your own finances and you are not a responsible payer. The court may also issue wage garnishment or an order that requires your company to send a portion of your salary to the credit card company that filed the lawsuit as payment for your debt.

This is not only embarrassing, it also leaves you with no control over your own income, forcing you to make do with what is left.

Effects on life in general

Spending a lot of time and energy buying things that you do not really need, thinking about shopping, returning items, hiding from your spouse, juggling multiple credit cards, hiding from credit card companies and bill collectors, and doing whatever it is that people with credit card addiction and huge debts do, can affect you personally. Your life seems meaningless because it revolves around material things. Your life becomes less productive and it gives you less satisfaction, which ultimately makes you unhappy.

Another effect of your credit card addiction and debt is bankruptcy. Filing for bankruptcy protects people with huge debt and help them pay off their debts the best possible way. There are three kinds of bankruptcy that individuals and businesses can file— Chapter 7, 11, and 13. Filing for bankruptcy is never easy. It is a long and tedious process that stays in your credit history even after you have paid off all your credit card debts.

Speaking of credit history, not paying your debts can have adverse effects on your credit reports. It is important to take care of your credit because this helps you a lot in life. You will find it easier to find a job, buy a house or car, or rent an apartment if you have a good credit standing. When applying for utility services, you may also be required to pay for a security deposit if you have a bad credit standing.

It is also more difficult to apply for a cell phone contract because cell phone companies also rely on your credit history to know if you are a good payer. Insurance companies may also increase your premium because they believe that people with lower credit scores are more likely to file for claims, maybe because accidents and delinquent accounts are both signs of irresponsibility.

Other side effects of your credit card addiction include getting evicted from your apartment because of consecutive late payments or receiving a foreclosure notice because you are not able to pay your mortgage. These scenarios can leave you with no place to stay, which is a sad thing, especially if you have little kids, because it is not their fault yet they are also suffering from your bad spending habits.

Hopefully, this chapter will convince you to stop your excessive credit card usage and pay off your debts now before it gets so bad that you have to file for bankruptcy or leave your home and live on the streets. You have to act now before it is too late! The following chapters will provide you with some helpful tips and solutions for stopping your credit card addiction and eliminating debt for good.

Chapter 5: Short-Term Solutions To Stop Credit Card Addiction

You first need to know some short-term solutions that can help you treat your credit card addiction. These will help you overcome those urges to shop using your credit card. You can turn some of these into habits that can ultimately help you eliminate debt. It is important to stick to these tips and strategies if you want to get positive results.

The first few days or even weeks can really be difficult and will really test your willpower and discipline. However, if you really want to overcome your credit card addiction and get rid of debt, then you need to be consistent in doing the solutions presented in this chapter. Here are some short-term strategies that can help you get rid of debt and stop credit card addiction.

Cut up your credit card

This is the title of this book and this ultimate act of letting go of your beloved credit cards can change your excessive spending habits that put you in too much debt. Some people simply put their credit cards inside the freezer and leave them inside a block of ice while other simply put their credit card at the bottom of their sock drawer. For people who have credit card addiction, these strategies may not work because they still have ways to access the credit card.

They can simply use a hammer to break the ice and get their credit card or they can just rummage through their sock drawer whenever they have the urge to shop. This is why the best tip is to just cut your credit card in half because no store in this world will accept a cut up credit card. One important thing to remember though is to avoid closing your account because this can do damage to your credit report.

Make shopping lists

You have to develop the habit of making a shopping list to prevent yourself from overspending. When you bring a list every time you go shopping, you are more likely to stick to your budget because you have a guide that helps you stay on track. For example, if you are buying groceries, you should make a grocery list of all the things that you need to buy and their corresponding prices.

Your list will prevent you from looking around and compulsively buying things that catch your attention. Creating shopping lists does not only apply to grocery shopping. You can also do the same thing when buying clothes for your family, office supplies, books, gifts, and so on.

Leave your wallet behind

If you love the experience of browsing through different shops and looking at their colorful displays, but you always end up buying things that you do not really need, then you should consider leaving your wallet behind and go window shopping instead. This way, you have no way to pay for items, thereby preventing you from buying anything. You can browse through different shops all you want without feeling stressed out and anxious, because there is no need to control yourself and your urge to buy since you do not have your wallet with you.

Find an alternative

You can replace your compulsive shopping behavior with something else to distract yourself from using your credit card and spending money on things that you do not really need in your life. Instead of shopping, you should instead indulge in something that requires little to no money such as reading in the library, going for a walk or jog, hanging out with friends at home, volunteering, watching your favorite movies online, and other more positive behaviors that can help you forget about your shopping and spending urges.

You can also decide to go back to school or enroll in a class to learn something new. You may need to spend money on these activities, but at least you are using your money for something worthwhile. You can also do this once you have paid off your debt and you are back on your feet again.

Avoid unnecessary temptations

Although it is a great idea to just leave your wallet at home if you want to visit your favorite shops, it is even better to just simply avoid being near these temptations that may trigger your desire to go shopping and use your credit card. If you can help it, do not go to shopping malls, discount warehouses and other places that will attract you to buy. You should not visit shopping websites and you should also throw away any shopping catalogues where you might find something that you absolutely must buy.

When you travel to other places, do not splurge too much on shopping for souvenirs or exotic items that you do not really like. If you want to have a lot of souvenirs, then you should take a lot of pictures instead; these are absolutely free!

Analyze your spending habits

You also need to analyze your regular spending habits so you will have a clearer idea where your money goes. Maybe a huge portion of your income goes to something that you really do not need like clothes and shoes. If this is the case, then you need to change your spending habits. Analyzing your spending habits will give you an idea of how to budget your money. You should compare your expenses for at least three months so you will know which items are recurring and necessary, like utility bills, which items are non-recurring but are important, like emergency spending, and which items are not really necessary, like clothes and bags.

If your income is higher than your expenses, then it means that you are still doing great. If your expenses are higher than your income, then it means that you are in debt and you need to do something about it right away. You can also check for patterns when you analyze your spending habits. Your regular payments should be consistent every month, like your mortgage and insurance premiums. If you can see a sudden increase in unnecessary purchases for the last couple of months or so, then you need to nip it in the bud before it turns into a full-blown compulsive shopping addiction.

Chapter 6: Long-Term Solutions To Stop Credit Card Addiction

Aside from short-term solutions, you also need to think about long-term solutions that can stop your credit card addiction for good. These long-term solutions will prevent you from going back to your old spending ways. Long-term strategies offer permanent solutions to your problem. Below is a list of long-term solutions that you can try to stop credit card addiction and eliminate debt.

Find a support group

Support groups are helpful because they surround you with people who are experiencing the same thing or have been there and have successfully overcome their credit card addiction and are now living a debt-free life. You can listen to some inspirational stories from these people that will motivate you to finally cut your credit card and eliminate debt. Support groups for shopaholics and spenders are very much the same as support groups for alcoholics or substance abusers. You can open up in front of these people and share your own experiences. You can tell them what you are going through when you feel ready to talk about it.

Contrary to what others think, support groups are not formal and intimidating. In fact, they are very casual so that members can relax and just simply be themselves. It is just like hanging out with a group of friends who are facing the same challenges in life. You can attend meetings even after you have treated your addiction and you have paid off all your debts to become an inspiration to others who are also in debt and to keep yourself from going back to your old ways.

Seek a therapist

Credit card addiction is the same as other types of addictive behaviors because they are all deeply rooted issues with causes. It is important to understand the reason why you are doing this particular behavior for you to be able to know how it can be properly treated. Your therapist can help you find the root cause of your credit card addiction. It could be that shopping takes your mind off your problems or you feel an adrenaline rush every time you hear the sound of the cash register and smell of new clothes.

Some people also experience a sense of accomplishment from being able to "save" money buying from sales and bargains, even though they are actually wasting their money because they often buy unnecessary items. There are also shopaholics who simply have a penchant for a particular object, like clothes, shoes, or gadgets.

Whatever the reason is, it is easier to understand your behavior once you get to the bottom of it. You will find out all about this with the help of a psychiatrist. Do not be afraid to ask for help because this is their job and they have probably dealt with people who are in worse situations.

Talk to a financial adviser

Aside from a psychiatrist who can help you understand the reason behind your addictive behavior, you should also consider talking to a financial counselor who can help you with your debt and your finances. You may need to pay a professional fee, but you can get expert advice and help from someone who knows the ins and outs of credit cards and debts. Your financial adviser can help you discuss the best possible payment plan with your creditors that can help you pay off your credit with the least possible damage.

The counselor can also face bill collectors who keep calling your number. This will at least make you feel less scared and panicked because someone who is more knowledgeable in this matter is handling your affairs. Your financial counselor can help you come up with a financial strategy that can help you get back up on your feet again and live a life free from debts and unnecessary financial obligations.

Just keep in mind that hiring a financial counselor does not mean that you will leave everything up to them. You still have to make the final and important decisions so that you will learn from your experience and you will never find yourself in the same situation ever again. It is also important to choose a financial counselor whom you are comfortable with because you are going to tell them confidential financial matters.

Set goals

People who waste money most likely do not have goals that guide them and keep them on track. This is just like creating a shopping list. Your goals will prevent you from spending unnecessarily because you have a target that you need to achieve. You can write financial goals like the ones in the list below:

- Pay off all your debt in five years' time.
- Save 10% of your income for savings.

- Save another 10% for your emergency funds.
- Buy a new outfit only once a month.
- Pay the utility bills on time to avoid late fees.
- Write down everything you need and make a trip to the grocery store only once a week. Be sure to stick to your budget.
- Set aside money for an annual vacation with your whole family.

These are some examples of financial goals that you need to do to prevent yourself from buying things that you do not really need and to curb your impulse to use your credit card. By setting goals, you have an idea where and how you want to spend your money. This will make it more difficult for you to spend unnecessarily, especially if your goals are tied up to your family's happiness and well being.

Live minimally

It may be difficult for someone who is used to spending money and accumulating a lot of stuff, but this is an effective way to curb your tendency to waste money. If you live minimally, you will find your life is happier and more fulfilling because you can now focus on things that really matter such as family, health, peace of mind, and happiness instead of material things. You can start living minimally by purging all the things that you do not need in your house and focusing only on your basic needs. If you realize how very little you need to live happy and comfortably, then you will be less tempted to spend money using either cash or credit card.

Chapter 7: More Tips For Paying Off Your Credit Card Debt

Stopping your credit card addiction can ultimately lead you to a debt-free life. You also need to find ways that can help you pay off your debt. Here are some more tips that will help you pay off your credit card debt:

Do it one card at a time

If you own multiple credit cards, then you will feel overwhelmed if you decide to pay off all of them at once. Instead of trying to pay off all your credit cards at once, you should instead target one card at a time. Focus all your efforts and payments first on the card that carries the lowest balance. Once you have paid off this card, you will feel good about your strategy and you will be motivated to do the same thing for all your other cards. Paying off the card with the lowest balance will also boost your credit standing right away instead of waiting for years to pay off all of them.

Request for low interest rates

People get in too much debt because of the large interest rates that credit card companies charge to their customers. This is especially true if you make a habit of making only minimum payments every month. It will seem like your balance is not going down even if you are paying the minimum every month. This is because of the high interest rate that can reach as high as 30%. You can request your creditor to lower your interest rates, which can instantly save you several dollars a month.

Although your credit history and your history with the lender play an important role in deciding your interest rates, it is still worth a shot. Sometimes, all it takes is a phone call and a polite request to lower your interest rate by several points. If you already have bad credit history and your account is already considered delinquent, you can ask a financial advisor to talk to your creditor or collection agency and request for a lower interest rate. They will be more willing to negotiate if they know that you are taking the necessary steps and you are serious about paying off your debt by hiring a financial adviser.

Consider balance transfers

This is something that you should do with caution. You should also avoid making a habit out of this tip. Do not transfer your balance to another credit card only to use up the credits in your cleared card once again. You should only transfer your balance from a credit card with high interest rate to a card with lower interest rate if you really intend to pay off your debt. This is because the low interest rates offered for balance transfers usually have a timeframe that lasts for 12 to 18 months.

You should also know that you will be charged a fee for transferring your balance. Despite this, you will still be better off in the end because of the lower interest rates, as long as you do it properly. Just make sure to leave the credit card that you have transferred the balance from with zero balance and focus on the credit card where you have consolidated all your debts.

Borrow money from another lender

You may think that this tip goes against the purpose of this whole book, but this can help you pay off your debt, especially when you have just started to be more financially responsible. If you really cannot get your payment from your income, you should consider borrowing money from a lender that offers fixed low interest rates. You can borrow money from this lender and pay off your credit card that has a much larger interest rate. This way, the interest that you need to pay for your loan will be so much lower.

Just like in the previous tip, you should also do this properly and you should not make this a habit. You need to pay off this new loan with a lower interest rate on time if you want to be debt-free. You can also borrow money from a family member or a friend. Just be sure to keep your promise of paying them on your specified date or your relationship will be affected. Do not use your credit card and leave it at zero balance.

Always pay on time

Later payments lead to penalties. You need to pay your credit card bills on time to avoid late fees that are also included in your total balance and are therefore charged interest. Late payment is also reflected in your credit report, especially if you do this more than once. Always make an effort to make your payment on time, even if you are just paying the minimum to avoid late charges that can add up to your total debt amount.

Find another source of income

This is ideally the best way to pay off your debt instead of balance transfers or borrowing money from another lender. However, not everyone has the time to get another job. If you are lucky enough to find another job, then you can use your extra earnings to pay off your debt and to start saving money. There are a lot of part-time jobs that you can apply for like online jobs or you can start your own small business at home.

Chapter 8: Improving Your Credit Without Credit Cards

The whole point of this book is to cut up your credit card and stop using it to treat your credit card addiction and to eliminate your debt. However, you need to improve your credit standing and having credit is one way to do it. However, how are you going to do it if you are not going to use your credit card? Although you are advised to cut up your credit card so that you can no longer use it, you should not close your account because it will look bad in your credit history. Just leave it open, but without any balance on it.

Below is a list of tips on how you can improve your credit without using your credit card.

Put utility bills in your name

Utility companies like Internet providers, phone companies, electric bill, and so on also report their customers' payments to the credit agencies. Before, they used to report only delinquent accounts that they have passed on to collection agencies, which is not exactly good for your credit history. However, today, they report all payments, especially major utility providers. You should call your utility company to check if they report your payments to the credit agencies. If not, you can always request a reference letter from them in case you need proof that you are a good payer.

Report your rent

TransUnion and Experian now include rent payments in their credit reports. You can have your rent payment included in your credit report via third party services like WilliamPaid, RentalKharma, or RentReporters. The charge is usually $10 or they sometimes offer their services for free as long as you pay your rent directly from your bank account using their website. Your rent payments do not affect your credit score, but they appear in your credit report.

Apply for a secured credit card

One important thing to understand before you react against this tip is that secured credit cards are different from traditional credit cards. It is secured because you have to make a cash deposit which prevents you from acquiring debt. Your cash deposit serves as your collateral. You still need to pay the balance in your secured credit card every month like you would a regular credit card.

The main difference is that there is a guaranteed cash deposit in case you are not able to pay your monthly payment. Your credit limit is determined by the amount of cash that you have deposited on your account. If you have deposited $1000, then this will be your credit limit and you cannot go beyond this amount.

This is different from a debit card because debit cards are simply linked to your bank account and your savings go down every time you make a purchase using your debit card. You should choose a card from a company that reports your credit card usage and behavior to any one or all three of the credit bureaus.

Open a regular savings account

Bank accounts in good standing prove that you know how to handle your finances. This can give you better opportunities with financers and lenders. They do not really affect your credit score, but they may reflect in your credit report.

Pay your bills on time

This cannot be stressed enough because late payments show how bad you are at managing your finances. If you want utility companies, financial institutions, and other third party services to submit glowing payment reports to the three credit bureaus, then you need to pay your bills on time at all times. They may give you a chance and not report your late payment if it only happens once, but if you make a habit out of it and your account becomes delinquent, then you can be sure that the company will report it to the credit bureaus.

You need to remember that it is more likely that your late payments will be reported than the payments you make on on time, so be sure to always pay your bills on time.

Conclusion

Thank you again for purchasing this book!

I hope this book was able to help you to learn some useful tips and strategies on how to stop your credit card addiction and be debt-free for life.

The next step is to use what you have learned in this book to help you become more financially stable and secure. You do not want your debt to get in the way of living a happy and peaceful life.

Thank you and good luck!

www.ingramcontent.com/pod-product-compliance
Lightning Source LLC
Chambersburg PA
CBHW070720180526
45167CB00004B/1561